M000291208

Financing a

Home

By Marc Robinson

 TIME LIFE ®
BOOKS

Alexandria, Virginia

State Street Global Advisors: educating people about money

For 200 years, we have been in the banking business helping people manage and invest their money. We are a global leader in the investment management industry, serving institutions and individuals worldwide.

Our goal in creating this series is to give you unbiased, useful information that will help you manage your money. No product advertisements. No sales pitches. Just straightforward, understandable information.

Our ultimate hope is that after reading these books you feel more informed, more in control of your money, and perhaps most importantly, more able to successfully plan and reach your financial goals.

Time-Life Books is a division of
TIME LIFE INCORPORATED

Time-Life Custom Publishing
Vice President and Publisher: Terry Newell
Director of Sales: Neil Levin
Director, New Business Development: Phyllis A. Gardner
Senior Art Director: Christopher M. Register
Managing Editor: Donia Ann Steele
Production Manager: Carolyn Bounds
Quality Assurance Manager: James D. King

© 1996 Top Down

All rights reserved. No part of this book may be reproduced in any form or by any electronic or mechanical means, including information storage and retrieval devices or systems, without prior written permission from the publisher, except that brief passages may be quoted for reviews.

First Printing. PRINTED IN U.S.A.

Time Life is a registered trademark of Time Warner Inc. U.S.A.

Books produced by Time-Life Custom Publishing are available at special bulk discount for promotional and premium use. Custom adaptations can also be created to meet your specific marketing goals.

Call 1-800-323-5255

**For State Street Global Advisors,
The Lab:**
Clark Kellogg
Jenny Phillips
Sally Nellson
Paul Schwartz

For Top Down:
Marc Robinson
Mark Shepherd
Research: Richard Kroll

The information contained in this publication is general in nature and is not intended to provide advice, guidance or expertise of any nature regarding financial or investment decisions. Neither Time-Life Books, State Street Bank and Trust Company, Marc Robinson, or Top Down make any representations or warranties with respect to the professional experience or credentials of the authors or contributors, or to the merits of the information of material contained herein. The reader should consult independent financial advisors and investment professionals prior to making any decision or plan.

Robinson, Marc, 1955-
    Financing a home : it's just what you need to know / by Marc
  Robinson
       p. cm. -- (Time Life Books your money matters)
    ISBN 0-7835-4790-0
    1. Mortgage loans--United States. 2. House buying--Costs.
I. Title. II. Series.
HG2040.5. U5R634 1996
332.7'22'0973--dc20
                       95-43386
                      CIP

Contents

The big picture

Like it or not, you're not just buying a home. You're the focus—and the starting point—of a global financial ecosystem where everyone depends on everyone else for survival. Since few of the people involved ever meet one another, most are forced to rely on detailed documentatic proving that you and the home are a sound investment. The mortgage process may seem rigid at times, but the rules allow you to have access to more mortgage money than home buyers have anywhere else in the world. The strict safeguards are the reason why lenders make you do the things you do.

Borrowers

These are people like you, the home buyer, needing to borrow cash to pay the seller. As you'll see, your payments become someone else's steady income.

You take a loan to give the seller the cash. A lender gives you the loan and expects to be repaid regularly with interest.

Lenders

Lenders can be banks, S&Ls, credit unions, and other institutions. Sometimes, they keep the loan and profit from the interest and fees you pay. Often, to replenish their stockpile of money to lend, they sell the loan to an investor, keeping the up-front fees as the profit.

Lenders sell loans to replenish their cash and make more loans. Packagers buy the loans, keep some, and bundle the rest into large packages.

Small investors

Small investors want a relatively safe place to earn steady income. For example, you might buy an insurance policy or shares in a mutual fund for the income it produces. Some of that income comes from investments in home mortgages. In fact, some of it might actually come from your own mortgage payments.

Individuals, like you, look for relatively safe investments—like a home mortgage. Large investors attract small investors with prospects of steady income.

Large investors

The reliable stream of payments is a good source of steady income and helps investors plan cash flows.

Insurance companies invest their premiums in loans, and pension funds invest employees' retirement savings, because loans are relatively safe investments. Many mutual funds invest in home mortgages either as their main strategy or as part of another strategy. Companies worldwide buy loans for their own accounts to help with cash flow and pay for construction projects, ongoing administration, and other business practices.

Large investors buy the packages to earn the interest you pay. Packagers sell the packages with guarantees.

Packagers

These huge financial institutions, such as FNMA ("Fannie Mae") and FHMC ("Freddie Mac"), keep money flowing from around the world to American home buyers. They buy loans, bundle them into huge packages ($500 million+ is common), and sell them with guarantees to large investors. (If you fail to repay your loan, the packager will pay investors and take the loss.) The packages are called mortgage-backed securities (investments backed by the terms of your mortgage agreement and loan note).

You're encouraged to buy

Owning a home is the American Dream for good reasons. It's good for:
- society (cleaner, safer neighborhoods);
- family (the security may motivate you to raise one);
- business (borrowing and building support many industries. Homeowners also have more to [lose] than renters by missing payments, and that may lead to better work habits and productivity);
- the economy (borrowing draws money from all over the world and keeps it circulating freely [).]

[**And the government offers some help.**]

They subsidize your expenses

You can usually spend more on a mortgage than you can on rent because you get a big tax break for owning a home. In effect, the government subsidizes your monthly mortgage payments based on your federal tax bracket. For example, if your mortgage is $1,500 a month, your after-tax payment would look like this:

Your tax bracket	The subsidy
39.6%	39.6% of $1,500 = $594
36%	36% of $1,500 = $540
31%	31% of $1,500 = $465
28%	28% of $1,500 = $420
15%	15% of $1,500 = $225

Your tax bracket	Your actual cost
39.6%	$1,500 - $594 = $906
36%	$1,500 - $540 = $960
31%	$1,500 - $465 = $1,035
28%	$1,500 - $420 = $1,080
15%	$1,500 - $225 = $1,275

Based on the table above, if you're in the 31% federal tax bracket, the government lets you take $465 of tax money and use it for housing costs. So, subtract that $465 from the $1,500 and your actual cost would be $1,035.

You take the subsidy in installments

You can adjust the withholdings on your W-4 form to increase your take-home pay and take advantage of the tax break every month instead of receiving it as a one-time tax refund. Ask your accountant for assistance; but here's the place to start:

The government lets you take "allowances" for each dependent you claim. You also can take another allowance if you claim yourself as "head of household," and another if you're claiming dependent care credit. You'll find a worksheet on the back of a W-4 that shows you, step-by-step, how to calculate your allowances (and increase your take-home pay) to include estimated mortgage interest and property tax payments.

Federal Housing Administration (FHA)

They don't lend money. They insure loans that meet specific guidelines. If you default, the FHA will pay the lender up to $91,950 for a loan on a single-family home (the 1995 limit). You pay the premiums: some up front and a monthly amount with your mortgage.

Farmers Home Administration (FmHA)

They help buyers in low-population areas get home loans. They also:

- make direct loans under strict guidelines to those who can't get a mortgage from a lender. The interest rate is based on what you can afford;

- guarantee up to 90% of a loan issued by a lender.

Veterans Administration (VA)

They guarantee loans to veterans of combat (and some noncombat) service. Eligibility requires an honorable discharge. If you fail to repay the loan, the VA will make up some or all of the payment to the lender.

State programs

Many states have special assistance programs for low-income and first-time buyers. HUD (Department of Housing and Urban Development) provides support for low-income housing and can steer you to any special programs in your area. Call 1-800-245-2691 for a program in your area.

Who buys homes { In 1994, first-time buyers accounted for 47.1% of home sales. Single, never-married buyers accounted for 17.7%, an historically high number.

More tax breaks { Since "points" are an up-front interest payment, they're also deductible. So are property taxes. Be sure to take your tax breaks for these expenses as well.

How much can you afford?

You'll want to know how much you can afford to spend. Lenders will want to know how much you can afford to repay when they lend you money for a mortgage. To that end, you have two resources and one limitation. In other words:

it all depends on your cash, income, and debt

Your cash for a down payment

The more savings you can put toward a down payment, the more loan options you'll have. Even without cash, however, you still may have options—depending on your circumstances.

0%: If you're a veteran with an honorable discharge, you may be eligible for a VA (Veterans Administration) loan. You may also pay lower fees and a lower-than-usual interest rate. If you live in a rural area and are a first-time buyer with low income, you may be eligible for a loan guaranteed by the FmHA (Farmers Home Administration).

3-5%: If you meet the low income requirements, you may be eligible for a loan insured by the FHA (Federal Housing Administration) or a loan through a state-sponsored program. Fannie Mae (the largest investor in home loans) offers a "3-2" option loan: You can put down 3% and get a gift or a grant for the other 2%.

6-19%: This is enough to qualify for a conventional loan, although you may be offered slightly more expensive terms. If you're in the under-20% range, you'll also be asked to buy private mortgage insurance (PMI), which protects the lender in case you default. At the closing you'll pay a one-year reserve of PMI up front, then a monthly premium. The PMI, therefore, will absorb some of your cash and affect your monthly payments. (When the difference between the value of your home and what you owe safely exceeds 20%, you may request an end to mortgage insurance.)

20%+: You can demand the best terms because you're a borrower in demand. (Lenders believe buyers with this much of their own money invested are the most likely to repay the loan.)

[About one-third of all buyers lack the cash to make a 20% down payment.]

Your income vs. monthly housing expense

Lenders will consider how large a house payment your income can support.

Housing expenses shouldn't exceed 25% to 28% of your gross monthly income *(not of your take-home pay).*

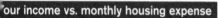

Housing expenses are the:

mortgage payment (principal and interest)

property taxes

home insurance

PMI (private mortgage insurance, if you put down less than 20%)

Include all other long-term debt

Then lenders will add the other long-term, steady debt you've committed to repay.

The total of your housing and long-term expenses shouldn't exceed 33% to 36% of your gross monthly income. Long-term debt means anything that will take at least 10 months to repay, such as:

car and student loans

child support

large, revolving credit bills

These are rules-of-thumb

The guidelines explained here are not hard-and-fast rules. Lenders will loosen or tighten them depending on other factors in your financial picture. For example, the amount of cash you'll put down, the reliability of your income, and whether your loan will be insured or guaranteed may all play a role in the lender's decision.

The contingency clause { Many people protect themselves by adding a clause to their contract with the seller that gives them the right to back out (and have their deposit returned) if they can't find a lender willing to make a loan at specific terms.

Prequalifying you *and* the lender

Lenders offer a service that's designed to advise you on how large a loan they could make. It's called prequalification—a valuable, easy, and quick service. And it's free, because it's a marketing tool. You're not obligated to use a lender who prequalifies you—no matter what a lender might say. As you would do when shopping for anything important, you're simply looking and learning; collecting information that will help find the right lender for you.

Each of you sees a financial overview

Often, you can walk right in and sit with a loan officer. (Who's going to turn down a potential customer?) The officer will ask you to estimate (as best you can, for your own benefit):

- the amount of cash you plan to use as a down payment;

- your gross monthly income from all sources;

- your monthly debt.

Based on the lender's current loan rates and fees, the loan officer will give you an estimated price range on homes you can afford, and an estimate of monthly payments, including the mortgage, insurance, property taxes, and more.

You benefit

1. By telling home sellers you're pre-qualified, you gain instant credibility and have more leverage to bargain for a better price.

2. You can learn about a lender's loan requirements: Is there a penalty if you pay off the loan ahead of schedule (prepayment penalty)? What other fees are there? Will you have to carry life or disability insurance? How much will you have to deposit into a special reserve (escrow) account at the closing to cover taxes, home insurance, or other charges? Will you have to pay the lender's attorney's fee?

3. You're in control. You decide whether or not the lender is the right fit for you.

Lenders benefit

1. They can begin to establish a relationship. By knowing some of your finances, they can now target you for other marketing efforts.

2. Better yet, they can try to make you a customer. For example, most banks give you a better mortgage rate if you have a checking account there.

3. They can save time and money by stopping applications from people who can't afford a loan.

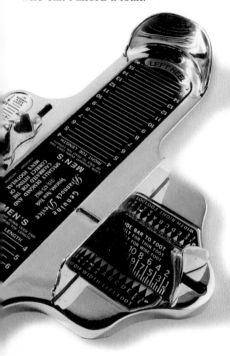

[*Where to borrow*]

Retail banks
They lend their own money and, therefore, set their own guidelines for approval. Approval is often quicker, rates a little higher, and down payment requirements a little steeper.

Credit unions
They lend only to members but otherwise offer the same advantages and disadvantages as retail banks.

Mortgage bankers
Strictly in the business of mortgages, they set the prices, process the application, fund the closing costs, then sell the loan to investors. Often they're affiliated with major, cash-rich corporations.

Insurance companies
They're major lenders who often target larger loans. (Also, if you have a whole life policy, you may be able to borrow against its cash value at a low rate. Ask your insurer.)

Lenders of last resort
Some companies offer extremely high rates and tough terms to buyers with poor financial histories.

Items lenders don't volunteer

Lenders are required to disclose information once you've applied. That's too late, however, to help your loan selection. For example, it helps to know:

The finance charge

your total cost of interest and fees over the life of the loan—to help you compare different loans.

The rate lock-in

to see what it would cost if you wanted to lock in the current interest rate until closing. Also ask how many weeks it should take to process your loan.

Understanding the marketplace

Ads are simply a way for lenders to attract your attention in a crowded, competitive marketplace. To attract as many—and as many different kinds of—customers as possible, lenders mix and match features to offer many variations on the theme.

Lenders know that many people look only for a low interest rate because they don't understand the other parts of a loan. There's more, however, to pay attention to.

Here's what } some lenders are saying:

NO POINTS

| 6.56% FIXED | 7.07% APR |

LOW RATES
4.75%   8.20%APR

Keep your cash . . .
Avoid up-front interest charges (points) you'll pay as a fee to the lender. But expect a higher rate and higher monthly payments.

. . . or make low monthly payments.
Pay more points and you can lower your payments. (If the APR is much higher than the interest rate, this may indicate that the lender is charging a lot of up-front fees.)

Take a chance . . .
Go for the lowest possible rate now and hope that rates don't rise substantially at each adjustment.

. . . Or play it safe.
Get a rate you know you can afford now; and you'll be able to plan your future finances around it.

We're not so strict;
and we'll approve quickly.
There's not much paperwork or many questions. Consider this if you need to close quickly or can't prove you have enough income. But expect to pay for the privilege in up-front cash or a higher rate.

1 year adjustable	3 year adjustable
4.50% 7.41% APR	5.87% 8.11%APR
30 year fixed	5 year adjustable
7.31% 7.69%APR	6.05% 7.91%APR

NO INCOME VERIFICATION LOANS

Low Annual

30 year fixed

6.2% 6.85%APR

Hareison Federal Bank

Term

The length of the loan. The longer you take to repay, the smaller each payment will be— but the more expensive the overall loan will be since you'll make many more interest payments.

Interest rate

Your annual fee for borrowing. It determines the amount of interest you'll pay at each installment.

APR (Annual Percentage Rate)

Required by law. A more accurate expression of your yearly cost of borrowing because it takes into account more than just the interest rate. APR combines the interest, the points, and other costs such as credit report fee, any mortgage insurance, and origination fees; then spreads that cost over the life of the loan (for example, 30 years).

Points

More interest. The amount you pay up front. One point equals 1% of the loan amount, so points can be expensive and absorb a large part of your cash. Technically, they're called "discount points," since the more you pay, the more of a discount you'll get on the interest rate. There may also be an "origination fee" (the commission for bringing in the loan) built into the points. Ask whether this fee is included in the points you're quoted.

30 Year Fixed

7.5% 7.85%APR
$6.99 per $1,000

15 Year Fixed

7.125% 7.5%APR
$9.06 per $1,000

Stretch payments . . .

Spread them over the longest possible time (30 years). You'll repay the loan slowly, pay much more interest overall, but each payment will be as low as possible.

. . . or repay quickly.

You'll have higher monthly payments, but more of each payment will go toward repaying your loan. That means you'll be building equity faster.

A good place to start shopping

Many newspapers show a table like this every week. It's a good place to watch rate trends, compare the competition, and call for application kits. Also ask your broker, lawyer, or friend for recommendations.

Mortgage Rate Report

Interest Rates for Purchases of Owners-Occupied, Single Family Homes*

30-Year Fixed

Lender	Phone No.	Type	TimesLine Access Code	Conforming Up to $203,150				Jumbo Over $203,150				Maximum Loan Amt.
				Interest Rate	Points	A.P.R.	Monthly Pmt. per $1,000	Interest Rate	Points	A.P.R.	Monthly Pmt. per $1,000	($000)
American Savings Bank	800-562-6272	S1	*2214	7.750	1.500	7.944	7.16	8.000	2.125	8.258	7.34	650
Bank of America	800-556-7811	B1	*2206	7.875	2.000	8.312	7.25	8.250	2.250	8.526	7.51	600
California Federal Bank	800-225-3337	S1	*2212	7.750	1.875	7.984	7.16	8.250	1.750	8.471	7.51	650
Chase Manhattan	800-586-2648	B1	*2217	NA	NA	NA	NA	8.063	2.500	8.364	7.38	1,000
Chase Manhattan Mtg.	800-900-6062	K3	*2226	7.750	1.625	8.142	7.16	8.125	2.250	8.399	7.42	300
Countrywide Funding	800-877-5626	K3	*2201	7.750	1.500	8.128	7.16	8.000	1.625	8.204	7.34	1,000
Downey Savings & Loan	800-336-9639	S1	*2227	7.625	2.375	7.911	7.08	8.000	2.250	8.272	7.34	650
First Federal Bank of CA	800-572-4332	S1	*2208	7.625	2.125	7.884	7.08	8.125	1.625	8.330	7.42	400
Fleet Mortgage Corp.	800-700-5650	K3	*2225	7.625	2.500	7.925	7.08	8.125	2.375	8.413	7.42	500

15-Year Fixed

Lender	Phone No.	Type	Access	Conforming				Jumbo				
American Savings Bank	800-562-6272	S1	*2214	7.250	1.500	7.553	9.13	7.625	1.500	7.920	9.34	65
Bank of America	800-556-7811	B1	*2206	7.375	2.000	8.053	9.20	7.625	2.125	8.026	9.34	60
California Federal Bank	800-225-3337	S1	*2212	7.250	1.875	7.615	9.13	7.750	2.000	8.131	9.41	65
Chase Manhattan	800-586-2648	B1	*2217	NA	NA	NA	NA	7.563	2.500	8.027	9.31	*1,00

What else will this cost?

It's a good idea to prepare early for the many expenses involved in buying a home. Costs usua range from 2% to 6% of the loan amount (expect the higher end if you're paying a few points). Once you apply, some of the fees will be nonrefundable.

Here are many of the FEES you're likely to face:

At application

Origination fee. Often included in the "points." This may be a flat fee or a percentage of the mortgage. It may go to the mortgage broker, if you use one. (Ask whether it's refundable if you don't close.)

Credit report fee. Covers the cost of reports on everyone who is responsible for repaying the loan.

Application fee. For processing the mortgage application.

Appraisal fee. The lender will hire an appraiser to estimate the value of the home.

$40–$75

$0–$350

$200–$300

At the closing

To Escrow:

These are payments to a neutral third party who will keep and distribute them when the payments are due. The lender should be able to estimate these costs at the time you apply.

Annual taxes such as property taxes, school taxes, and municipal taxes. You will have to pay the amount due for the remainder of the year.

Private mortgage insurance (PMI). If you default on the loan, the lender will be protected. These premiums continue until you owe less than 80% of the home's value. The premiums usually are added to any amount you must escrow for taxes and homeowner's insurance.

Homeowner's insurance. Most lenders require you to prepay the first year's premium and bring proof of payment to the closing. This protects them even if the house is destroyed.

$100-$1000

To Third Parties:

Title search costs. Your attorney can recommend a title company and advise you of the cost.

Attorney fees. Either a percentage of the loan, flat fee, or hourly rate.

$200-$500 — **Lender's attorney's fee.** Expect to pay it.

$50-$250 — **Document preparation fees.** A way for lenders to add a little profit. Try to negotiate this away. May be included in attorney's fee.

$50-$75 — **Preparation of amortization schedule.** A good document to have, so you can see how much you've repaid at any given time—and know how much to prepay if you so choose.

$150-$350 — **Title insurance.** A one-time premium, paid at closing, plus a monthly amount added to the mortgage. It covers the lender in case there is a legal problem or a creditor's claim against the property.

$200-$300 — **Inspections required by lender.** These can vary. It may be a termite inspection or a water test, for example.

To the Government:

$20-$30 — **Recording fees.** For the county clerk to file the deed and change the property tax billing information.

Prepaid interest. Interest on your loan for the remaining days of the month.

Transfer taxes. Required in some places to transfer the title and deed from the seller to you. Other state and local fees may apply.

To the Seller:

The cash down payment. Whatever you still owe, after your deposit.

Seller reimbursements. To pay for the days you'll be receiving services, like gardening and trash collection, for which the seller has already paid.

To the Lender:

Points. A point is equal to 1% of the amount borrowed. For FHA and VA mortgages the seller, not the buyer, must pay it. Some lenders will let you finance points, adding the cost to the monthly payments. Points paid up front are tax deductible.

[*For Your Benefit*]

You may want to spend a little extra for these:

Inspections. In addition to inspections required by the lender, you may make the sale dependent on satisfactory completion of certain inspections (e.g., structural, water quality, radon). Who pays the fees is negotiable.

Owner's title insurance. You may want to purchase title insurance so that if problems arise, you're not left owing loan payments on property where ownership is disputed. A thorough title search (going as far back as 1900) can assure a clear title. Cost: $150-$300.

Appraisal fees. For a "second opinion," you may want to hire your own appraiser, especially if the lender's appraisal isn't satisfactory. Cost: $200-$300.

What lenders want to know about *you*

It's time to get your ducks in a row. Do this quickly and get it right because:

1] You're trying to reassure lots of people you'll never meet, and they'll want details, on the record.

2] The longer it takes to be approved, the more chance for problems to arise (for example, your interest rate could rise while you wait, or there could be new property damage).

Lenders want you to *prove you have:*

Enough cash

Where do you have it?

You'll need to show enough to cover the down payment, fees, closing costs, and moving expenses. Collect the last three months' statements for every bank, mutual fund and brokerage account. Prove you've used some cash for the deposit: Get your bank to send you the cancelled check immediately.

Is it still there?

The lender asks each firm to verify current balances and average balances for the last two (and maybe up to six) months.

Is it all yours?

Relatives or close friends may give you a cash gift, but you'll need to prove it's:

- specifically for the down payment;
- not a loan (which would add to your debt—not your assets);
- in your account, available for use.

Good credit

How do you handle your debts?

You'll need to prove you've been a good borrower in the past. Collect information from your credit card statements and other documents to provide the following:

- each credit card, account number, address, and what you owe;
- any open credit lines from lenders like your bank;
- any loans (e.g., auto, education) and amounts owed;
- any legal judgments against you.

Have you had problems?

The lender will send for your credit report and may ask you to explain any problems.

What do you earn?

You'll also need to show your ability to pay what you borrow. Include your last two pay stubs. The lender will send a verification form to all employers from the last two years, and ask your current employer about:

any time spent unemployed (not fatal unless unusual);

likelihood of pay raises;

consistency of bonuses, commissions, overtime;

likelihood of continued employment.

Any other steady income?

Include year-end statements and other documents that prove:

income from securities or a trust (show two years' tax returns);

Social Security, disability, alimony and/or child support (voluntary; only if you want it considered);

rental income (a lease agreement).

What's your tax picture?

Show your last two income tax reports— the ultimate proof of your earning power.

Other documents to send
- Copy of the full contract
- Attorneys' and brokers' names, addresses, phones

Follow up on employers
Many don't answer the verification forms without prompting. That can delay your entire application process.

Cash from your 401(k)
You may typically borrow up to 50% of the amount vested (the amount you could take if you left the company today). Ask your company's benefits department for details.

If you're self-employed
Include a profit-and-loss statement for the year-to-date, tax returns from the last two years, a year-to-date balance sheet prepared by an accountant, and any contracts that show future income. Even though you could lose money for tax purposes and still run a successful business, most lenders will want to see actual net income (not explanations of how tax savvy you are).

City	1992	1993	1994
Memphis	1.5	1.6	2.2
Minneapolis	1.7	2.3	2.0
New York	4.2	4.7	4.2
San Francisco	4.9	4.1	3.0

Average years for first-time buyers to save for a down payment:

SOURCE: CHICAGO TITLE AND TRUST COMPANIES

Lenders must keep you informed

Lenders are legally required to give you certain information. These papers and pamphlets may look boringly official, but many are surprisingly well-written. Most important of all - - - - - -

they explain what to expect and what rights you have.

The Equal Credit Opportunity Act Statement

Lenders may not discriminate for any reason that is covered by federal law, including race, sex, or religion.

Good Faith Estimate of Closing Costs

(Also called "settlement costs.")
You must receive this within three business days of applying. Some lenders include it in the application kit. The figures may not be 100% precise, since costs are subject to marketplace changes, but they must be reasonably close to what you'll actually pay. The estimate isn't a guarantee.

Truth-in-Lending Statement

You must receive this within three business days of applying. Among the information provided are:

Finance charge. Pay attention to this line. It shows how much you'll pay over the life of the loan.

Amount financed. The amount you'll borrow.

Late charges. The fee for payments made beyond a certain grace period.

Prepayment. Whether or not you're entitled to make early or extra payments or to repay the entire loan ahead of schedule.

Loan Disclosure

This form shows how an ARM (or some other complex kind of loan) works.

Lock-in and Processing Disclosures

The interest rate quoted when you apply may change by the time you go to closing. Lenders want the rate to "float" so they don't commit a low rate, then, weeks later, make your loan when rates could be much higher. The Rate Lock-in Disclosure details how much you may pay to lock in the current rate for various lengths of time. Compare the rate-lock with the lender's Loan Processing Disclosure, which estimates how long it'll take to process your loan: Could your rate-lock expire before you have time to go to closing?

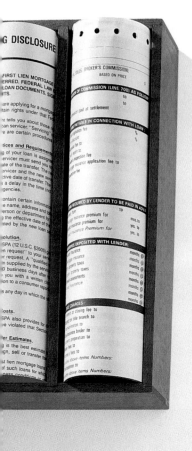

Right to Receive Appraisal Copy

Many states give you the right to see the appraisal that was used to determine the value of your new home. Request it from the lender in writing.

HUD-1 Settlement Statement

A two-page list of all the services provided and what you'll pay for them at closing. You're entitled to see the actual amounts one business day ahead of the closing. (Ask your attorney or the lender to show you.) In states with "escrow closings"—where you don't go to an actual closing—you'll receive the statement after you close.

Servicing Disclosure

Lenders often transfer the servicing of your loan (for example, collecting payments, sending statements, and handling escrow payments) to another company. This form says you must be notified by the lender and the new servicer within 15 days of the transfer (with exceptions), and that both must include toll-free numbers. During the first 60 days after the transfer, you have extra protection: For example, any payment you make to the lender by accident can't be treated as a late payment by the new servicer.

A Consumer Handbook on Adjustable Rate Mortgages

Only for ARM borrowers, this booklet comes with a form to sign stating that you received it.

You have the right to complain }

Start with the party you think created the problem. The Department of Housing and Urban Development (HUD) also encourages you to send complaints to:
**U.S. Department of Housing and Urban Development
Director, Office of Insured Single Family Housing
Attention: RESPA
451 Seventh Street, SW
Washington, DC 20410**
HUD wants you to know that your complaints can lay the foundation for future legislative actions.

The credit report

Lenders use a credit report to verify the information you've provided. The report isn't subjective; it includes no opinions or judgments. It's strictly a factual account of your borrowing and payment habits. Credit reports are provided by credit bureaus. Formats will vary, but essentially, each report *provides information from public records and businesses.*

Read the report

The information in the report shown here is fairly typical. Many credit bureaus have redesigned their report formats to be easily understood. Reports typically include the account, the date it was opened, the number of months reviewed, when you last used the credit, the most you've borrowed, and current status. A memo usually accompanies your report explaining any codes or other shorthand the bureau uses.

You will also see a list of "inquiries." This means you'll see the name of anyone who has requested a look at your credit report during the last two years.

You can order a report

You're legally entitled, for a small fee, to see everything in your credit report—and to know how it got there. In fact, many people order a report before they apply for a loan, just in case there are mistakes or problems that could be resolved before a lender sees them.

When it's free

If you've been denied credit, you're entitled to a written explanation from the lender. If the reason involves your credit report, you're entitled to a free copy from the credit bureau, as long as you make the request within 60 days.

If you think something in your report is wrong or deserves an explanation, you can have the credit bureau check it. Send your request in writing. Within approximately 30 days, the bureau will verify the information and send you the results. If you still have a dispute, you may include a written statement (100 words or less) in your credit file.

Who to **contact**

There are thousands of local bureaus across the country; check your local listings. These small bureaus are connected to one of three national credit networks that collect the data. You may contact them at:

TRW: 800-422-4879

Equifax: 800-685-1111

Trans Union: 718-459-1800

There is also a national consumer organization willing to help:

National Foundation for Consumer Credit: 800-388-2227

With over two million pieces of information pouring into credit bureaus daily, errors are inevitable. Some may end up on your report.

Common errors

1 Confusing you with someone else who has the same name or a similar Social Security number.
2 Failing to remove negative information after the issue is resolved.
3 Failing to incorporate your comments into the file.

Is the property worth it?

It depends whether you're the lender or the borrower. You're both looking at the home as an investment. You both want to minimize your risks, but that means something different to each of you. The focal point of the investment is the difference between the loan amount and the home's market value. The question is,

Is there enough **CUSHION** *in the deal?*

The Equity

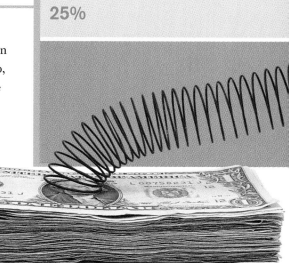

25%

When you buy a home, you're thinking of living in it, not selling. But if and when you sell it, you hope to make a profit. So, you look at the cushion and estimate the amount of money that will go into your pocket after repaying what you owe. To you, therefore, the difference between what you owe and the potential sales price of your home is your equity.

In this example:
At the start, you make a down payment (put down $25,000). You borrow the rest (take a $75,000 loan). Your equity = 25% (of the $100,000 home value).

The loan amount: $75,000

The loan amount is the amount you owe.

● How does it go down?

You pay off your loan (the principal).

● How does it go up?

You borrow more.

The market value: $100,000

Market value is the estimated price you'd receive if you sold the home.

How can it go up?

You put in improvements (for example, upgrade the kitchen).

Inflation raises the price of everything.

Real estate values increase in the area.

How can it go down?

You let your home fall into disrepair.

Real estate values fall in your area.

75% →

The **Loan-to-Value**

Lenders aren't worried about your profit; they just want to be repaid, earn a profit from the interest, and avoid taking a loss. So they look at the cushion between the loan amount and the home's market value and call it, appropriately, the loan-to-value ratio. The wider the gap between the loan amount and the value of the home, the smaller the loan-to-value ratio (which is good for the lender). For example, if the lender lends you $75,000 on a $100,000 home, the loan-to-value ratio is 75%. That's better for the lender than giving you a $85,000 loan, (a loan-to-value ratio of 85%) because it would be easier to get back the loan amount if the home had to be sold in foreclosure.

In this example:
At the start, they give you a loan ($75,000).
They appraise the market value ($100,000).
Their loan-to-value = 75%

the loan

> Both you and the lender will hope the market value goes up and you regularly repay the loan, so that the loan amount goes down. The faster you repay the loan, the faster you increase your equity and profit potential; and the lender decreases the loan-to-value and lowers the risk.

The approval process

When the loan officer has all your documents, the loan package is sent to the underwriter (the one who approves or rejects it based on predetermined guidelines). If this person works for the lender, your loan officer may have some influence over the decision. If, however, the underwriter works for the ultimate investor, the decision may be more cut-and-dried. Here, generally, is

how underwriters analyze you and the home against the terms of your loan request.

A **cash** cushion

Large cash reserves and/or a large down payment can help overcome doubts about your ability to meet monthly payments. Conversely, if your cash is unimpressive, you could be asked to accept a higher rate. (This could be good for the lender because the higher-than-normal interest you'd pay could induce investors to buy your loan at a premium.)

Steady **income**

If you'll be left with little cash, your income becomes more important. Underwriters will be cautious if your income is volatile (for example, based on commissions, bonuses, or royalties), you're self-employed, or your employment has been unsteady.

Any **credit** problems

An underwriter may grade you this way:

A No more than two late payments *reported* in the last 12 months. No major credit problems in the last five years.

B A few late payments reported in the last 12 months, but no major problems in the last five years.

C A serious problem (e.g., a car loan or a credit card revoked) within the last five years. Approval is possible but you may be asked to accept less favorable terms.

D Several serious problems or a bankruptcy within the last five years. Approval is still possible but at the most restrictive terms.

The home's market **value**

Even if you pass muster, the home must be worth the loan. Otherwise, there's the risk that you may default and leave creditors with property that can't be sold for a satisfactory price.

Delays could cause problems

's common for lenders to ask for more
nformation to help the underwriter seal any
oles. Repeated requests, however, may signal
lelays. Typically, it takes about four to five weeks
o collect all the information; and it should take
he underwriter only about another week to
nalyze your application and make a decision.
After that, the closing can happen as soon as
veryone is able to coordinate schedules.

Vhen you prequalify or apply, be sure to
sk how long the process should take. If you
nd that it actually is taking longer, consider
nvolving your lawyer or complaining up the
hain of command—because time can definitely
ost you money.

If you're approved

You'll receive a commitment, usually
in writing. More than just a notice, the
commitment may also require you to make
some quick decisions:

Tasks: Sometimes commitments are condi-
tional, requiring you to resolve certain open
issues before the lender will go to closing.

Options: You may be offered some choices
to go forward. One popular option also
available when you apply is the rate-lock.
A rate-lock is like an extended warranty: For
a certain period—possibly 30 to 60 days—
you're guaranteed the quoted rate even if
rates rise. (Get it in writing.) Otherwise your
rate will float (fluctuate until the closing).

Time: Be sure that your contract with the
seller (or a feature like a rate-lock) won't
expire before you can go to closing.

If you're rejected

You're entitled to ask for detailed, written
reasons. Some may be correctable; some
may not be so serious to other lenders.

Ask if you could be approved for a loan
that wouldn't be sold to an investor (and
therefore wouldn't need to meet the same
requirements).

Consider reapplying elsewhere (and
address the problems openly with the new
lender). You'll lose the fees for the credit
report, appraisal, and any other nonrefund-
ables. However, the points, including an
origination fee, should be returned to you.
When you go to prequalify or apply, be
sure to ask what fees are refundable.

The closing

This is the culmination, the official meeting of the interested parties. In some states, there are no face-to-face closings; it's all handled by mail through an escrow agent (a neutral third party). In most states, though, you'll go to an actual closing,

where everyone is paid and protected.

Before you go: prepare

1. Confirm the right time and place.

2. Walk through the home to make sure all is as it should be.

3. Review with your attorney the exact closing costs.

4. Get certified or bank checks for certain costs, such as the points and the rest of the down payment. (No bounced or stopped checks allowed.)

5. Bring with you:

   Checkbook to cover unexpected expenses.

   Power of Attorney, notarized and signed by any co-owners who won't be there. This document gives you authority to sign for them.

   Proof of mortgage insurance (if you've had to buy it).

   Proof of home insurance.

Who will be there

The most likely candidates are:

You and your attorney: To sign checks and documents, and protect your interests.

The seller and attorney: They do the same for themselves.

Settlement attorney: In some deals a neutral party coordinates the closing.

The lender's representative: To receive fees, make the loan, and protect their interests.

The title company or escrow company representative: To raise and help solve outstanding issues, and collect any money for the reserve account.

The real estate broker(s): To collect the commission, and sometimes help solve problems or disputes. (Some of the money may not be distributed until a few days after the closing.)

Ways to save on title costs { If the seller owned the home for only a few years, the seller's title company may give you a "reissue rate" for title insurance. Your attorney may also receive discounts from a favorite title company.

Beware last-minute switches { If the lender surprises you with a higher rate, more points, or other fees, get your attorney involved. that doesn't work, contact the lender's top management and your state's mortgage banker's association after the closing.

You budgeted the cash for up-front expenses and convinced the lender you had enough cash, and now it's time to prove it. You go down the checklist on the HUD-1 Settlement Statement and write and distribute the checks.

To the lender

Pay the points and fees. Your first regular mortgage payment actually begins at the end of the next month—because each payment covers the previous month. So, you'll live in the home a month before making your first payment. (Interest on the loan begins immediately.)

To the seller

Pay any down payment remaining, any other agreed-upon expenses such as items you bought (e.g., curtains and lights), and any adjustments for monthly gas and electric bills.

To escrow

To assure the lender that certain future bills will be paid, you'll pay money to the escrow agent. This person is responsible for holding the money in an escrow (reserve) account and distributing it to the proper places when the bills are due. Typical escrow payments include up to a year's worth of property taxes, mortgage insurance premiums (if any), and home insurance premiums. Other escrow payments could cover disputed repair bills or estimates, and any special assessments.

The person representing you should review each document carefully and explain its significance before asking you to sign it. Here are some of the highlights of what you'll be asked to do:

Promise to repay the loan

The loan note and mortgage agreement represent your promise to repay the loan and your pledge that, if you fail, the lender is authorized to sell your home to recoup the money.

Clear up outstanding issues

The title company's search of public records will show any liens filed against the property (disputes over unpaid bills or even over ownership). Unpaid taxes or repair bills and property line disputes are a few examples. A search may also uncover claims against someone else with your name— and you'll be asked to verify your lack of involvement.

Transfer ownership

The seller gives you the deed: the official document that transfers ownership.

27

The mortgage agreement

For lenders and investors, this is the key. The loan note and mortgage agreement create your promise to repay the loan. Since their purpose is to lay out all the terms in detail, they tend to be filled with dense, legal language.

In essence, it all works out to four questions:

How much will you **borrow**?

The amount you borrow is called the principal (referred to in many documents as "amount financed"). Usually, you'll borrow the difference between your down payment and the sales price. If you don't have enough cash to pay the up-front fees, however, some lenders will add it to the loan amount. For example, you may need a $100,000 loan plus the cash to cover $3,000 in fees. The lender could give you a $103,000 loan; you'd give the seller $100,000 and give $3,000 right back to the lender to pay for the fees. It's a good deal if you need the cash. The downside is your monthly payments will be higher—because you borrowed more.

What will it **cost**?

The agreement will tell you the:

- interest rate you're agreeing to pay;
- total amount of interest over the life of the loan;
- total amount you will repay.

Don't forget, there are other associated expenses—home insurance and property taxes, to name two—that must be paid up-front before the lender will make the loan.

Compromise plans

Defaulting isn't always fatal. Lenders don't really want to force you out of your home, or be stuck trying to get back their money by foreclosing on (selling) your house. You may be able to arrange a compromise payment plan—if you can win back the lender's trust.

Short pay-off

If you default and you owe more than your home is worth, the lender may be willing to sell the home, take the money, and forgive the rest of the debt. This is called a short pay-off.

Late fees

You'll be charged for bounced checks or if your payment arrives more than 10 to 15 days after the due date. Defaulting may trigger a stiff penalty; for example, one lender charges 24% a year on the amount you owe until it's repaid—plus collection agency and legal fees.

What's the payment plan?

How many years may you take to repay the full loan? (Typically, 15, 20, or 30 years.) What's the installment plan? (Will you repay monthly, twice each month, or on another schedule?) Each of your payments includes principal and interest. Are these payments fixed (will they be the same every time) or will they be adjusted periodically? When will adjustments occur, how will they be calculated, what's the most your rate can go up or down each time, and what's the most it can ever go up? Most lenders let you make payments ahead of schedule, called prepayments. Some lenders limit what you can prepay or charge penalties. In many states, however, lenders are prohibited from restricting your prepayments. (You may always prepay an FHA-insured loan.)

What if you don't repay?

Failing to keep your promises can put you in default. Typically, you're in default if the lender doesn't receive payment within 30 days of the due date. If you're often late with payments or you don't maintain the home and it loses value, the lender may be able to force you to accelerate payments (repay the full loan immediately).

Security is crucial to the entire deal. The lender secures the loan with something of equal value: your home (called the collateral). This means the lender may sell your home if you default. It also means you've given the lender a sense of security—which makes it easier to say "yes."

Fixed & adjustable rate mortgages

Home loans fall into two main categories:
fixed rate mortgages and adjustable rate mortgages (ARMs).

One is simple and predictable; the other can *change* and involves a **formula**.

Fixed rate mortgage

This is the basic, straightforward loan. The interest rate is fixed for the life of the loan. You pay exactly the same principal and interest amount every time (except the last payment, which covers the uneven amount that remains).

A fixed rate mortgage provides peace of mind and predictability to home buyers because:

- their current income should always be able to cover the mortgage payment;

- they can plan their budgets every year more reliably.

Variations

Even these are basic. The standard length of time is 30 years. You have the option to own more of your home faster and to pay less overall interest, by compressing the length of the loan to 25, 20, 15, or even 10 years. You also have the option to raise or lower the payments by adjusting the up-front interest ("points") you'll pay. Once you make your selections, however, your payments remain fixed for the life of the loan.

Be aware

Many ARMs include benefits for lenders that may catch you off-guard if you're not aware of them.

Negative amortization. If your loan includes a "negative amortization" clause, you could make payments that don't cover the interest due, and will therefore cause your loan balance to increase instead of drop.

Teaser rates. Also called "initial interest rate." The opening rate is artificially low to entice you to borrow. Within the first few adjustments, it rises in line with current rates and could leave you with payments you can't afford.

Adjustable mortgage

Consider an ARM if you:

- can't afford payments on a fixed rate;

- want to gamble that rates will drop;

- plan to repay the loan before, in the worst-case scenario, it would adjust to the level of the current fixed rate.

What it is

A loan that starts at a lower rate than a fixed loan and then is adjusted periodically to keep it generally in line with interest rate trends in the economy.

How it works: The ARM formula

Your ARM comes with a formula used to determine how much your rate will rise or fall over the life of the loan. Lenders are legally required to give you information on how ARMs work. The example at right shows how to calculate a rate adjustment on a loan with a current rate of 6% and a cap of 2%.

1. Determine the size of the adjustment

How often. Payments will adjust periodically. Common are ARMs that adjust: every six months, 1 year, 3 years, 5 years or 7 years.

When it occurs. The rate change must be calculated before it's due to go into effect. Typically, it's 45 days ahead.

Find the index. Your loan is tied to the swings of another interest rate (or combination of rates), called the index. The lenders choose which index, but it must be outside their control and should be a rate you can follow in newspapers. The most common index is U.S. Treasuries
(e.g., 1-year T-bills) **6.75%**

Add a set amount. The lender then adds a margin (the predetermined percentage increase) to the index .... **+2.50%**

The adjusted rate **9.25%**

2. Limit the adjustment

Every ARM has protections built in for you.

Start with your current rate **6.00%**

Apply the cap. The cap is the most your rate can rise at each adjustment   **+2.00%**

Your new rate **8.00%**

Compare to the adjusted rate
(from above) .... **(9.25%)**

Hold at the cap **8.00%**
(see sidebar below)

The rate cap saves you **1.25%**

Stop at the ceiling { Also known as the lifetime cap, this is the most your rate can ever rise over the life of the loan. If your loan starts at 6% and the ceiling is 5%, your rate can never go above 11%.

Convert to a fixed { Some loans include a feature that lets you get out of the adjustment gamble and convert to a fixed-rate loan at certain times—for a fee or at a slightly higher rate.

Compare payments

Points, interest rates, term: What effect will these three variables have on the amounts you'll pay? Here, you can compare loans that vary the three options: One standard, one where you pay more up front to lower the monthly payments, and one you pay off in half the time.

Low cash up front and the longest payoff schedule

$100,000 loan at 8%, 30-year fixed, with one point paid up front. Monthly payment $734.

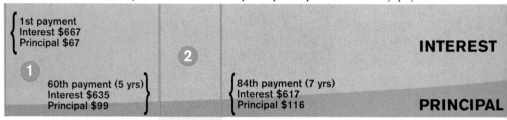

1st payment
Interest $667
Principal $67

60th payment (5 yrs)
Interest $635
Principal $99

84th payment (7 yrs)
Interest $617
Principal $116

INTEREST

PRINCIPAL

Year 15

More cash up front in exchange for lower interest

Three points paid up front and 7.5% interest. Monthly payment $699.

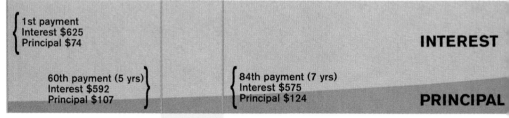

1st payment
Interest $625
Principal $74

60th payment (5 yrs)
Interest $592
Principal $107

84th payment (7 yrs)
Interest $575
Principal $124

INTEREST

PRINCIPAL

Year 15

Paying more each time but saving a lot in the long run

15-year fixed at 7.8%. Monthly payment $944.

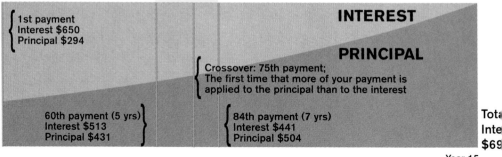

1st payment
Interest $650
Principal $294

INTEREST

PRINCIPAL

Crossover: 75th payment;
The first time that more of your payment is applied to the principal than to the interest

60th payment (5 yrs)
Interest $513
Principal $431

84th payment (7 yrs)
Interest $441
Principal $504

Tota
Inte
$69

Year 15

Notice three points:

1 In all loans, lenders front-load the interest so they can collect much of the overall interest even if you pay off the loan quickly.

2 The average buyer either sells the home or refinances within five to seven years (marked by the orange band), so consider how much you'll have paid off at that point.

3 The total interest you'd pay over the life of each loan.

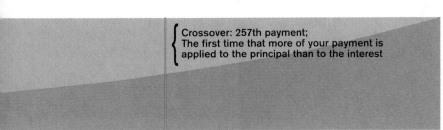

Crossover: 257th payment;
The first time that more of your payment is applied to the principal than to the interest

3

Total Interest: $164,160

Year 30

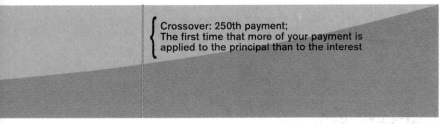

Crossover: 250th payment;
The first time that more of your payment is applied to the principal than to the interest

Total Interest: $151,722

Year 30

Add savings to any loan you choose

Adding an extra amount to every payment, or making even one extra payment a year, can create dramatic savings. The technique is called prepayment, and it's easy to do. Simply include a separate check and a note designating the extra money to pay off principal (the loan amount, not the interest).

For example, on a 15-year loan of $100,000 at 7.5% interest:

Prepayment: Add $25 to every payment.

Savings: $3,585 in interest over 15 years.

Timing: Own the home eight months ahead of schedule.

Who's who

Your real estate agent/broker
Your main relationship and a valuable resource—but brokers serve the seller's interests first: The seller pays them. If you reveal what you're willing to spend, your broker is obligated to tell the seller. Good sources for names of attorneys, mortgage brokers, or lenders. By law, they're not allowed to take a fee—or insist you take their recommendation.

Your attorney
Some states don't require one, but for first-time home buyers, an attorney may be worth the price. Fees are often a percentage of the sale price, but negotiable. The attorney should read every document (including the contract with the seller) before you sign and should be at the closing.

Mortgage brokers
Do the loan legwork and help find the right lender and loan. They know the mortgage market and have contact with many (but not all) lenders. Good ones can help speed the process. Not-so-good ones simply add a layer of bureaucracy and keep you from direct contact with the lender. Brokers often say they get better deals; verify that for yourself. Their fee is built into the points (usually the "origination fee" goes to the broker).

The appraiser
Hired by the lender; paid by you. Assesses the home's worth, based on its characteristics and location. This helps lenders avoid making unreasonably large loans.

The home inspector
Your hire. Analyzes the home's physical condition before you buy it: electrical, plumbing, and structural. If major problems you could try to renegotiate with the seller.

Mortgage insurance company
Insures the lender in case you default—even though you pay the premiums. Usually mandatory if your down payment is less than 20%.

Title company
Makes sure the seller owns the property and no one else has any claims against it, such as unpaid taxes, legal actions, creditor claims. Provides the lender with title insurance (paid by you or the seller; you could buy your own, too) in case problems arise after closing.

The loan servicer
Sometimes lenders sell the function of servicing a loan to another company. The servicer takes your payments, passes them through to investors, pays your insurance and taxes from escrow when due, sends you monthly statements and notices, and handles customer service.

The underwriter
The one (working for the lender) who analyzes your application based on pre-set guidelines, then rejects or approves.

[Appendix]-------→

Fixed rate and adjustable rate mortgages are the most common kinds of loans. Here are some—not all—of the many other options available from a competitive industry that's trying to find a way to make you a customer.

"No Documentation" Loan

Either a fixed or adjustable, this features a streamlined application process that requires fewer documents such as direct verification of employment. You're judged largely on your credit history (must be excellent) and the size of your down payment (must be large). This loan may carry a higher than usual rate.

Biweekly Mortgage

You make payments every two weeks instead of once a month—the equivalent of 13 monthly payments each year. Thus, you save a lot in interest over the life of the loan and build up equity faster.

Growing Equity Mortgage

A fixed rate loan with a rapid payoff schedule. Payments increase by a predetermined percentage, with the extra amount of each payment applied toward the loan's principal. A much less expensive loan, but your income must be able to handle the increases.

Two-Step Mortgage

The interest rate adjusts only once (e.g., at fi or seven years), then fixes at the market rate for the remaining years of a 30-year term.

Short-Term Balloon Mortgage

Aimed at buyers who expect to stay in thei homes only a short time. Payments are base on a 30-year term, so they're low, and you may also get a lower interest rate. But the fu loan balance is due in a shorter time, typica five or 10 years. At that point you must "ma a balloon payment" or refinance.

Graduated Payment Mortgage

The interest rate—and payments—start artificia low, so the loan is more affordable. Sometim only part of the interest is paid; the remainde is added to the outstanding balance, which is known as "negative amortization." This mort gage may also be obtained through a "buy-down," in which you pay points up front in exchange for the lower initial interest rate.

Casualty

Protects you against losses to your property, such as fire, theft, vandalism, and weather-related damages. This is what you need to prove you have before you can close on your mortgage.

Structural

Covers damage to the structures on your property, such as the home and an unattached garage. The coverage is based on the value of all structures within 100 feet of your house.

Landscaping

Covers landscape damage but limited to 5–10% of your structural coverage. Also limits coverage on specific trees and plants (in case there are unusually valuable ones).

Loss of Use

Provides living expenses when you can't live at home. Usually 10–20% of structural coverage.

Personal property

Covers all your furniture, jewelry, clothes, a other personal items. Usually up to 50% of t structural coverage.

Medical

Pays medical bills for someone injured on y property.

Liability

Covers personal liability to protect you in la suits from people injured on your property.

Umbrella liability

Links your car and home, so that you have one overall coverage. Also increases liability coverage on both.

Hurricane/Flood/Earthquake

Most policies cover wind, hail, and other weather conditions. But in areas susceptible catastrophic losses from nature, you'll often need to buy additional coverage.

MORTGAGE CHECKLIST

Complete this worksheet for each mortgage you're considering.
(Ask the lender for assistance, if necessary.)

	Mortgage A	Mortgage B
Loan amount	$_____	$_____
APR, if fixed rate loan	_____	_____
APR, if adjustable	_____	_____
Adjustment period	_____	_____
Index and current rate	_____	_____
Margin	_____	_____
Initial payment	_____	_____
Rate cap, each period	_____	_____
Lifetime cap	_____	_____
Negative amortization	_____	_____
Prepayment privilege	_____	_____
Initial fees and charges	_____	_____

Next year's payments, if:

	Mortgage A	Mortgage B
Index stays same	_____	_____
Index goes up 2%	_____	_____
Index goes down 2%	_____	_____

Make copies of this sheet, based on a form prepared by the
National Association of Realtors, and use it to rate and compare the
features of properties you are considering.

Is it the right house?

Total rooms____ Number of bedrooms____ Number of bathrooms____

Kitchen size and equipment	good____	average____	poor____
Size and shape of living spaces	good____	average____	poor____
Ventilation throughout house	good____	average____	poor____
Traffic flow between rooms	good____	average____	poor____
Storage (attic, closets, garage)	good____	average____	poor____
Owner and visitor parking space	good____	average____	poor____
Back/front yard maintenance level	easy____	average____	difficult____

Location, Location, Location

Travel to work	easy____	average____	difficult____
Travel to school	easy____	average____	difficult____
Public transportation	easy____	average____	difficult____
Schools	good____	average____	poor____
Stores	close____	average____	far____
Hospital	close____	average____	far____
Fire station	close____	average____	far____
Police station	close____	average____	far____
Public library	close____	average____	far____
Place of worship	close____	average____	far____
Post office	close____	average____	far____
Parks and recreation facilities	close____	average____	far____

se this checklist to assess the quality of any home that you're serious
)out buying.

ard

_ Ground level, well drained

_ Driveway smooth, not too steep

_ Established lawns or gardens

oundation

_ Basement not wet (look for stains, mildew, or decayed baseboards)

_ Wood not rotten

_ Slab level, not cracked

_ No large cracks in concrete or block

_ Floor insulated (at least 6 inches)

tructure

_ Walls straight, no major cracks or sags

_ Floors are level

_ Roof in adequate condition, not approaching wear-out

_ No water stains on ceilings or walls

_ Rafters don't sag

_ Visible joists and beams are undamaged

_ No daylight shining through attic ceiling

_ Chimneys aren't deteriorated

Exterior

___ Doors open easily, aren't rotten

___ Windows weatherproofed, not rotted

___ Paint not peeling or blistering

___ Gutters and drain pipes in place

Interior

___ House appears generally "well kept"

___ Furnace, air conditioner, water heater, and major appliances aren't overly aged

___ Floors don't creak badly or sag

___ Carpets not too worn or discolored

___ Electrical wiring not deteriorated

___ Electric service capacity is adequate

___ Circuits are not overfused

___ Kitchen and laundry room circuits are separate

___ Accessible outlets in every room

___ Good water pressure in all faucets (operate four or five at once to test)

___ Waste water drains quickly

___ Plumbing silent when water in use

___ No plumbing leaks around joints

___ Toilets don't "run," refill quickly and fully when flushed

Here are some government and private organizations willing to help.

Department of Housing and Urban Development (HUD)

451 7th Street, SW
Washington, DC 20410
Programs for low-income housing.
For program information: 202-708-4374
For the nearest HUD office: 202-708-1112

Department of Veterans Affairs (VA)

Loan Guarantee Service
Department of Veterans Affairs
810 Vermont Avenue, NW
Washington, DC 20420
Guarantees a portion of home loans made to veterans. Offers free publications on their programs. Also runs a low-financing program for non-veterans who are buying VA-acquired homes.
For information and phone numbers for local offices: 800-827-1000

Consumer Product Safety Commission

Washington, DC 20207
Accepts complaints about safety in areas such as smoke alarms and insulation. Provides safety tips.
Call 800-638-2772

Consumer Federation of America (CFA)

1424 16th Street NW, Suite 604
Washington, DC 20036
A group of pro-consumer organizations that lobbies for consumers in Washington. Reportedly has over 50 million members. Regularly publishes a newsletter.
Call 202-387-6121